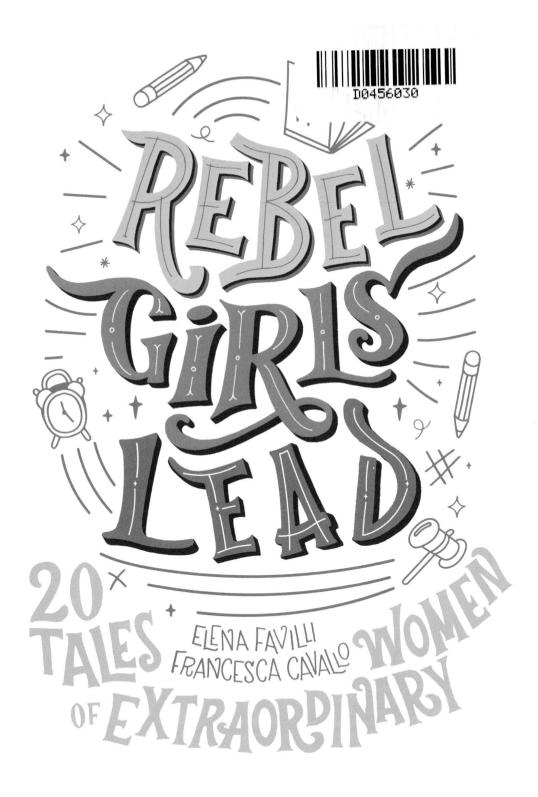

REBEL GiRLS LEAD

20 TALES OF EXTRAORDINARY WOMEN

ELENA FAVILLI
FRANCESCA CAVALLO

Parts of this work have been previously published in the books *Good Night Stories
for Rebel Girls* and *Good Night Stories for Rebel Girls 2*.

Created by Francesca Cavallo and Elena Favilli
Art Direction by Giulia Flamini
Graphic Design by Annalisa Ventura

ISBN: 978-1-338-56737-3

10 9 8 7 6 5 4 3   21 22 23

Printed in the U.S.A. 113

First Scholastic printing, September 2019

CONTENTS

ANGELA MERKEL   CHANCELLOR   1

CATHERINE THE GREAT   EMPRESS   3

CHRISTINA OF SWEDEN   QUEEN   5

CLEOPATRA   PHARAOH   7

ELIZABETH I   QUEEN   9

EUFROSINA CRUZ   ACTIVIST AND POLITICIAN   11

EVITA PERÓN   POLITICIAN   13

GIUSI NICOLINI   MAYOR   15

GRACE O'MALLEY   PIRATE   17

HARRIET TUBMAN   FREEDOM FIGHTER   19

HILLARY RODHAM CLINTON   PRESIDENTIAL CANDIDATE   21

LEYMAH GBOWEE   PEACE ACTIVIST   23

MALALA YOUSAFZAI   ACTIVIST   25

MICHELLE OBAMA   LAWYER AND FIRST LADY   27

NANNY OF THE MAROONS   QUEEN   29

RIGOBERTA MENCHÚ TUM   POLITICAL ACTIVIST   31

RUTH BADER GINSBURG   SUPREME COURT JUSTICE   33

SERAFINA BATTAGLIA   ANTI-MAFIA WITNESS   35

SOJOURNER TRUTH   ACTIVIST   37

YAA ASANTEWAA   WARRIOR QUEEN   39

ACTIVITIES   41

QUIZ   43

INTERVIEW WITH THE AUTHORS   46

WORKSHOP   48

ILLUSTRATORS   50

ABOUT THE AUTHORS   51

PREFACE

Dearest Rebel,

   With this book, we unravel the stories of powerful leaders past and present. You will right wrongs with political activist Rigoberta Menchú Tum, reveal difficult truths with witness Serafina Battaglia, and captain a fleet of ships with pirate Grace O'Malley. We celebrate the unreserved ambition that steered these women to become great leaders.
   Women are often the footnote (if mentioned at all!) in the historical record so do not be surprised if these names are new. Today, we put them front and center. Celebrate their accomplishments, and take this opportunity to investigate other hidden figures.
   Always remember that you are the lead character in your story. You are powerful. You are capable of being a strong leader. Speak your mind and fight for what you believe in, and like the women whose stories we've featured here, you will change the world.

Dream bigger, aim higher, fight harder, and when in doubt, remember you are right.

Rebel Girls

ANGELA MERKEL

Once upon a time, in Templin, Germany, there lived a seven-year-old girl called Angela. One Sunday, she was listening to her father's sermon in church when her mother started to cry.

"What's the matter?" Angela asked.

"They are going to build a wall," her mother said. "They want to seal off the border between East Germany and West Germany."

Angela was stunned. "Why would they build a wall?" she thought. "People should be free to go wherever they like."

Not only would East Germans be stopped from going to the West, but they would be barred from listening to the news coming from the other side.

Every day, Angela would hide in the school washroom with a little radio and try to catch a station from the West. It was illegal to do this, but she didn't care: she wanted to know what was happening to her country.

When Angela grew up, she studied quantum chemistry and wanted to become a university professor. The secret police told her that she would be promoted only if she spied for them. Angela refused, and she never became a professor.

She was working as a researcher in a lab when the Berlin Wall was demolished. She called her mom and said, "I think we're free to go to the West." Indeed, they were.

Angela eventually became chancellor of Germany—a determined leader who knew the pain walls could cause and never wanted her people to be divided again.

BORN JULY 17, 1954
GERMANY

"WHAT WE SEEK IS HARMONY AMONG NATIONS. THAT WAS AND REMAINS THE GREATEST GOAL OF EUROPEAN UNITY."
– ANGELA MERKEL

ILLUSTRATION BY
ELENIA BERETTA

CATHERINE THE GREAT

EMPRESS

Once there was a queen who disliked her husband. Her name was Catherine and her husband, Peter, was the emperor of Russia. The Russian people found him mean and arrogant.

Catherine knew she would do a better job of ruling the country. All she had to do was to figure out a way of replacing her husband.

Six months after becoming emperor, Peter went on vacation, leaving Catherine behind. This was her chance. Catherine gave a rousing speech to the royal soldiers to get them on her side. They switched their loyalty from Peter to Catherine, and a priest declared her the new ruler of Russia. She then ordered a suitably magnificent crown to be made.

One of her first acts as empress was to order her husband to be arrested and put in jail.

Catherine's magnificent crown took two months to create! It was made of gold and silver encrusted with 4,936 diamonds, 75 pearls, and a huge ruby on top.

During her reign, Catherine expanded the Russian empire, winning many wars and uprisings.

Lots of people were envious of this powerful woman. They said nasty things about her behind her back when she was alive, and when she died, they said she must have fallen off the toilet! In fact, she died in her bed and was buried in a golden tomb in Saints Peter and Paul Cathedral in Saint Petersburg.

MAY 2, 1729–NOVEMBER 17, 1796
RUSSIA

"I AM ONE OF THE PEOPLE WHO LOVE THE WHY OF THINGS."
—CATHERINE THE GREAT

ILLUSTRATION BY MARIJKE BUURLAGE

CHRISTINA OF SWEDEN

QUEEN

Once upon a time, there was a six-year-old queen. Her name was Christina, and she had succeeded her father on the throne upon his death.

Christina was smart and fiercely independent. Because she had a lot of responsibility on her shoulders, she knew she had to grow up fast, so she studied philosophy, art, foreign languages—and even ballet, to be able to move gracefully as a queen.

When Christina turned eighteen, everyone expected her to marry a suitable man from a noble family—someone to increase her power. But she was in love with one of her ladies-in-waiting, a young and beautiful woman called Ebba Sparre, and she had no interest in marriage.

After reigning for ten years, Christina shocked everyone by giving up the throne and moving to Rome. There, she had a wonderful time, making friends with artists, writers, scientists, and musicians from all over Europe. She realized that she missed being queen, however, and plotted to seize control of the Kingdom of Naples, but her plan quickly fell apart.

Pope Alexander VII called her "a queen without a realm, a Christian without faith, and a woman without shame," and he was right. Christina was never ashamed to show the world who she really was, even in the face of criticism. She was unconventional and she loved it. Thanks to her free spirit, she became one of the most influential women of her time.

In Rome, Christina formed the literary circle that gave rise to the Academy of Arcadia, an institute for literature and philosophy that exists to this day.

DECEMBER 8, 1626–APRIL 19, 1689
SWEDEN

"IT IS A FAR GREATER HAPPINESS
TO OBEY NO ONE THAN
TO RULE THE WHOLE WORLD."
– CHRISTINA OF SWEDEN

CLEOPATRA

PHARAOH

Once upon a time, in ancient Egypt, a pharaoh died and left his kingdom to his ten-year-old son, Ptolemy XIII, and to his eighteen-year-old daughter Cleopatra.

The two had such different ideas on how to run the country that soon Cleopatra was kicked out of the palace and a civil war broke out.

Julius Caesar, a great Roman general and politician, traveled to Egypt to help Cleopatra and Ptolemy find an agreement. "If only I could meet Caesar before my brother does," Cleopatra thought. "I could convince him that I'm the better pharaoh." But she had been banished from the palace. The guards would have blocked her at the entrance.

Cleopatra asked her servants to roll her up inside a carpet and smuggle her into Caesar's rooms. Impressed by her daring, Caesar restored Cleopatra to the throne. They became a couple and had a son. Cleopatra moved to Rome but then Caesar was killed, so she went back to Egypt.

The new Roman leader, Marc Antony, had heard a lot about this strong Egyptian queen and wanted to meet her. This time, she arrived on a golden barge, surrounded by precious jewels and silk.

It was love at first sight.

Cleopatra and Marc Antony were inseparable. They had three children and loved each other to the end of their lives.

When Cleopatra died, the empire ended with her. She was the last pharaoh to rule Ancient Egypt.

69 B.C.E.–AUGUST 12, 30 B.C.E.

EGYPT

ILLUSTRATION BY
KIKI LJUNG

"I WILL NOT BE
TRIUMPHED
OVER."
—CLEOPATRA

ELIZABETH I

QUEEN

Once upon a time, there was a king who wanted to leave his kingdom to a son.

When his wife gave birth to a daughter, King Henry VIII was so mad that he left her, sent the child away, and married another woman. He believed that only a man would be able to rule the country after he died, and was delighted when his new wife gave birth to a boy: Edward.

Henry's daughter, Elizabeth, grew up a bright and brilliant girl, with striking red hair and a fiery temper.

Edward was only nine when his father died and he became king. A few years later, he also became ill and died, and his sister Mary became queen. Mary thought that Elizabeth was plotting against her, so she locked Elizabeth up in the Tower of London.

One day, the Tower guards burst into her cell. "The queen is dead," they announced. And then they fell to their knees in front of her. Elizabeth instantly went from being a prisoner in the Tower to the country's new queen.

Elizabeth's court was home to musicians, poets, painters, and playwrights. The most famous was William Shakespeare, whose plays Elizabeth adored. She wore gowns decorated with pearls and lace. She never married; she valued her own independence as highly as that of her country.

Her people loved her dearly and, when she died, Londoners took the streets to mourn the greatest queen they had ever had.

SEPTEMBER 7, 1533–MARCH 24, 1603
ENGLAND

"A CLEAR AND
INNOCENT CONSCIENCE
FEARS NOTHING."
—ELIZABETH I

EUFROSINA CRUZ

Once there was a girl who didn't want to make tortillas.

When her father told her that women can only make tortillas and children, she burst into tears and promised to show him that it wasn't true. "You can leave this house, but don't expect a single cent from me," he told her.

Eufrosina started out by selling chewing gum and fruit on the street to pay for her studies. She got a degree in accounting and came back home with a job as a teacher. She started to teach young indigenous girls like herself, so they could also find the strength and the resources to build their own lives.

One day, she decided to run for mayor of her town. She won many votes, but despite that, the townsmen canceled the election. "A woman as mayor? Don't be ridiculous," they said.

Furious, Eufrosina started to work even harder. She founded an organization called QUIEGO, to help indigenous women fight for their rights. Their symbol was a white lily. "Wherever I go, I take this flower to remind people that indigenous women are exactly like that: natural, beautiful, and resilient," Eufrosina said.

A few years later, Eufrosina became the first indigenous woman to be elected president of the state congress. When the first lady of Mexico came to visit, Eufrosina walked arm-in-arm with her, in front of the local population.

She showed her father—and the whole world—that there is nothing that the strong, indigenous women of Mexico cannot do.

BORN JANUARY 1, 1979
MEXICO

"WHEN A WOMAN DECIDES TO CHANGE, EVERYTHING CHANGES AROUND HER."
—EUFROSINA CRUZ

ILLUSTRATION BY
PAOLA ROLLO

EVITA PERÓN

POLITICIAN

Once upon a time, in South America, lived a beautiful girl called Eva. As a child, Eva dreamed of escaping her life of poverty by becoming a famous actress and film star.

When she was just fifteen years old, Eva moved to the big city of Buenos Aires to pursue her dream. With her talent, good looks, and determination, she soon became a celebrated actress onstage and on the radio. But Eva wanted more: She wanted to help people less fortunate than herself.

One night, at a party, she met Colonel Juan Perón, a powerful politician. They fell in love and got married shortly after.

When Juan Perón was elected President of Argentina one year later, Eva quickly became known by her affectionate nickname: Evita. The people loved her passion and her commitment to helping the poor. She fought hard for women's rights and helped women win their right to vote.

She became such a legendary figure that she was asked to run as vice president to help govern alongside her husband. Although she was loved by the poor, many powerful people feared her charisma and power. "They just can't deal with a young, successful woman," she used to say.

After discovering she had a serious illness, Evita decided not to run, although she did help her husband win a second term as president. When she died, only a few months later, the announcement came on national radio: "We have lost the spiritual chief of our nation."

MAY 7, 1919–JULY 26, 1952
ARGENTINA

ILLUSTRATION BY
CRISTINA AMODEO

"YOU MUST WANT! YOU
HAVE THE RIGHT TO ASK!
YOU MUST DESIRE."
—EVITA PERÓN

GIUSI NICOLINI

MAYOR

There was a young woman named Giusi who loved the little island of Lampedusa, where she was born. Criminal groups and ruthless corporations wanted to destroy Lampedusa's pristine beaches to build hotels and vacation homes, but Giusi wouldn't let them.

As the director of Lampedusa's natural reserve, she said, "it is my duty to protect this island with all my might." Her enemies burned down her father's shop. "You will not intimidate me," she declared. Her car and her boyfriend's van were set on fire. "I will not back down!" she said.

Lampedusa is a tiny island in the Mediterranean Sea, between Europe and Africa. Many refugees who were fleeing Africa to escape war and build a better life in Europe landed there. The inhabitants of Lampedusa didn't know what to do. "Should we send these people back to protect our island?" they wondered. "Or should we welcome them?"

With these questions in mind, they went to vote for their next mayor.

Giusi was one of five candidates. People knew she had given all she had to protect the island in the past, so they wanted to hear what she thought about the current situation. Giusi explained her point of view with four simple words: "Protect people, not borders."

Lampedusans elected her.

As mayor, Giusi reorganized the island's immigration center to be able to welcome as many people as possible. "We want to see many boats on our shores," she insisted, "because that will mean that these people made it here and didn't drown."

BORN MARCH 5, 1961
ITALY

"IT'S NATURAL FOR AN ISLAND TO BE WELCOMING!"
— GIUSI NICOLINI

ILLUSTRATION BY LAURA PÉREZ

GRACE O'MALLEY

PIRATE

Once upon a time, on a wild green island, lived a girl with long ginger hair. Her name was Grace.

When wind howled and waves crashed against the rocks, Grace would stand on the clifftop and dream of sailing out across the stormy seas. "Girls cannot be sailors," her father told her. "And anyway, your long hair would get tangled in the rigging."

Grace didn't like this one bit. She cut her hair short and dressed in boy's clothes to prove to her family that she too could live the life of the sea.

Finally one day, her father agreed to take her sailing, on one condition: "If we meet a pirate ship, hide below deck," he said. But when they were attacked, Grace leaped off the rigging and landed on one of the pirates' backs! Her surprise attack worked—and they beat the pirates off.

Grace was a fine sailor and wanted to do something more exciting than catching fish. When the English attacked her castle, she became a pirate herself rather than submit to English rule. Grace was so successful that soon she had her own fleet of ships as well as several islands and castles along the west coast of Ireland.

When the English captured her sons, Grace sailed to meet the Queen of England, Elizabeth I, to try and save them. To everyone's surprise, the queen and Grace became friends. The queen returned her sons and possessions, and Grace helped her fight against England's enemies, the Spanish.

CIRCA 1530–1603
IRELAND

ILLUSTRATION BY
KATHRIN HONESTA

"I AM THE QUEEN
OF THE SEA."
—GRACE O'MALLEY

HARRIET TUBMAN

FREEDOM FIGHTER

One day, a girl was standing in front of a grocery store, when a black man came running past. He was being chased by a white man, who yelled, "Stop that man! He's my slave!"

She did nothing to stop him. The girl's name was Harriet, she was twelve years old, and she was also enslaved. Harriet hoped the man would escape. She wanted to help him.

Just then the overseer hurled an iron object at the running man. He missed, but hit Harriet on the head. She was badly injured but her thick hair cushioned the blow enough to save her life. "My hair had never been combed," she said, "and it stood out like a bushel basket."

A few years later, the family who owned her put her up for sale, so Harriet decided to escape.

She hid in the daytime and traveled by night. When she crossed the border into Pennsylvania, she realized for the first time in her life she was free. "I looked at my hands to see if I was the same person now that I was free. There was such glory over everything, and I felt like I was in heaven."

She thought about the runaway slave, and her family in Maryland who were still enslaved. She knew she had to help them. Over the next eleven years, she went back nineteen times and rescued hundreds of enslaved people.

She was never captured, and she never lost a single person.

CIRCA 1822–MARCH 10, 1913
UNITED STATES OF AMERICA

ILLUSTRATION BY
SALLY NIXON

"...AND I PRAYED TO GOD TO MAKE
ME STRONG AND ABLE TO FIGHT, AND
THAT'S WHAT I'VE ALWAYS PRAYED
FOR EVER SINCE."
—HARRIET TUBMAN

HILLARY RODHAM CLINTON

PRESIDENTIAL CANDIDATE

There was a time when only boys could be whatever they wanted: baseball players, doctors, judges, policemen, presidents.

At that time, in Illinois, a girl named Hillary was born.

Hillary was a brave, blond girl with thick glasses and boundless curiosity. She wanted to go out and explore the world, but she was scared of the rough boys in her neighborhood who laughed at her and called her names.

Once, her mother saw her hiding inside. "Hillary, you get out there and deal with them. Otherwise, the bullies will win without even a fight."

So out she went. She learned how to fight against bullies and soon found others who were fighting, too: people of color fighting against racism, single moms fighting to bring up their kids. Hillary listened to all their stories, and tried to figure out how she could help.

The best way to fight for justice, she decided, was to go into politics. Because many Americans were not used to seeing a woman politician, they criticized her for silly reasons, like her hairstyle, the sound of her voice, or the clothes she wore. They tried to bully her out of politics. But Hillary had learned how to deal with bullies, and she stood up to them.

Hillary became the first woman nominated by a major party for President of the United States.

There was a time when girls could not be whatever they wanted, but that time is gone.

BORN OCTOBER 26, 1947
UNITED STATES OF AMERICA

"TO EVERY LITTLE GIRL WHO
DREAMS BIG, I SAY: YES, YOU CAN
BE ANYTHING YOU WANT—EVEN
PRESIDENT."
—HILLARY RODHAM CLINTON

LEYMAH GBOWEE

PEACE ACTIVIST

Once, in Liberia, a woman stopped a war. Her name was Leymah, and she was a single mother of four. Her country was going through a violent civil war: children were being recruited as soldiers, and hundreds of thousands of people were dying. Leymah worked hard to help those who had been traumatized by the fighting.

One day, she was invited to a conference organized by the West Africa Network for Peacebuilding. "Women like me had come from almost all eighteen countries in West Africa," Leymah recalled.

At the conference, she learned about conflict and conflict resolution. The women shared their experiences and talked about what war had taken from their lives. For Leymah, it was enlightening. "No one else," she thought, "is doing this—focusing only on women and only on building peace."

She became the leader of a program called the Women in Peacebuilding Network. To recruit other women, she went to mosques for Friday afternoon prayers, to the markets on Saturday mornings, and to churches every Sunday. All the women she spoke to were tired of a war they had never wanted in the first place—a war that was killing their children.

Leymah and the other women in her network pressured the factions at war to start peace talks. Then they gathered in front of the hotel where the negotiations were taking place to demand rapid progress. They even blocked the hotel exit to keep the negotiators from leaving until they had reached a deal.

When the Liberian civil war ended, Leymah was awarded a Nobel Peace Prize. "When women gather," she says, "great things will happen."

BORN FEBRUARY 1, 1972

LIBERIA

ILLUSTRATION BY
THANDIWE TSHABALALA

"WE MUST CONTINUE TO UNITE IN
SISTERHOOD TO TURN
OUR TEARS INTO TRIUMPH."
– LEYMAH GBOWEE

MALALA YOUSAFZAI

ACTIVIST

Once there was a girl who loved school. Her name was Malala. Malala lived in a peaceful valley in Pakistan. One day, a group of armed men called the Taliban took control of the valley. They frightened people with their guns.

The Taliban forbade girls from going to school. Many people disagreed but they thought it would be safer to keep their girls at home.

Malala thought this was unfair, and wrote about it online. She loved school very much—so one day, she said on TV, "Education is power for women. The Taliban are closing girls' schools because they don't want women to be powerful."

A few days later, Malala got onto her school bus as usual. Suddenly, two Taliban men stopped the bus and shouted, "Which one of you is Malala?"

When her friends looked at her, the men fired their guns, hitting her in the head.

Malala was rushed to hospital, and she did not die. Thousands of children sent her get well cards, and she recovered faster than anyone could have imagined.

"They thought bullets would silence us, but they failed," she said. "Let us pick up our books and our pens. They are our most powerful weapons. One child, one teacher, one book, and one pen can change the world."

Malala is the youngest person ever to receive the Nobel Peace Prize.

BORN JULY 12, 1997
PAKISTAN

"WHEN THE WHOLE WORLD IS SILENT, EVEN ONE VOICE BECOMES POWERFUL."
—MALALA YOUSAFZAI

ILLUSTRATION BY SARA BONDI

MICHELLE OBAMA

LAWYER AND FIRST LADY

Once upon a time, there was a girl who was always afraid. Her name was Michelle Robinson and she lived in a one-bedroom apartment in Chicago with her family.

"Maybe I'm not smart enough. Maybe I'm not good enough," she worried. And her mother would say, "If it can be done, you can do it."

"Anything is possible," said her dad.

Michelle worked hard. Sometimes, teachers told her she should not aim too high because her grades were not that good. Some people said she would never achieve something big, because "she was just a black girl from the South Side of Chicago."

But Michelle chose to listen to her parents. "Anything is possible," she thought. So she graduated from Harvard and became a lawyer at a big firm. One day, her boss asked her to mentor a young lawyer. His name was Barack Hussein Obama.

They fell in love and got married a few years later.

One day, Barack told her he wanted to become President of the United States. At first, she thought he was crazy, but then she remembered: "If it can be done, you can do it." So she quit her job and helped him on his campaign.

Barack won the election (twice!), and Michelle became the first African-American First Lady of the United States. "No one is born smart. You become smart through hard work," is her motto.

BORN JANUARY 17, 1964
UNITED STATES OF AMERICA

ILLUSTRATION BY
MARTA SIGNORI

"ALWAYS STAY TRUE TO YOURSELF AND
NEVER LET WHAT SOMEBODY ELSE SAYS
DISTRACT YOU FROM YOUR GOALS."
—MICHELLE OBAMA

NANNY OF THE MAROONS

QUEEN

Once upon a time, in Jamaica, there lived an escaped slave with royal African ancestors. Her name was Queen Nanny, and she was the leader of a group of escaped slaves called the Maroons.

At the time, Jamaica was occupied by the British. They enslaved Africans and deported them to Jamaica to work on sugarcane plantations. But Queen Nanny wanted freedom for herself and for her people, so she escaped, freed many other slaves, and led them into the mountains where they built a village called Nanny Town.

The only way to Nanny Town was along a narrow path through the jungle. Queen Nanny taught the Maroons to cover themselves with leaves and branches to blend in with the jungle.

As British soldiers walked through the forest in single file, they had no idea they were surrounded. But at the sound of a signal, the "trees" around them suddenly leaped to life and attacked.

Nanny Town had one problem, though. Its inhabitants were hungry.

One night, weak with hunger and worried for her people, Queen Nanny fell asleep. She dreamed of one of her ancestors who told her: "Don't give up. Food is at hand."

When she woke up, she found pumpkin seeds in her pockets. She planted them on the hillside and soon her tribe had plenty of food.

From then on, the hill near Nanny Town was called Pumpkin Hill.

CIRCA 1686–1733
JAMAICA

ILLUSTRATION BY
CAMILLA PERKINS

"I AM FREE NOW."
—NANNY OF THE MAROONS

RIGOBERTA MENCHÚ TUM

POLITICAL ACTIVIST

Once there was a girl who was told she didn't matter. She lived high in the mountains of Guatemala, but she and her family had to work down in the valleys picking coffee beans. The plantation owners worked them hard and beat them if they did not pick fast enough. The workers were treated like slaves and were paid hardly anything. "Your life is not worth a bag of beans," her bosses told her.

"My name is Rigoberta," she replied, "and my life is worth just as much as yours."

Rigoberta was proud of her people and her culture. The Mayans of Guatemala could trace their history back to ancient times. They had a rich and wonderful civilization. But they had been forced into poverty, and they were beaten and even killed by soldiers if they dared to protest.

She started fighting for better conditions and equal rights for her people. She organized strikes and demonstrations. Although Rigoberta could not read or write, she spoke with such conviction that more and more people joined her cause. Many were taken away and killed, including Rigoberta's own parents and her brother. The government tried to silence her and the landowners tried to break her, but no one could crush her fearless spirit. She insisted on telling her story—not because it was hers but because it was the story of oppressed indigenous peoples everywhere.

Rigoberta played a large part in ending the civil war in Guatemala. For this, and for her life's work campaigning for the rights of the poor, she was awarded a Nobel Peace Prize.

BORN JANUARY 9, 1959
GUATEMALA

"I AM LIKE A DROP OF WATER ON A ROCK.
AFTER DRIP, DRIP, DRIPPING IN THE SAME PLACE,
I BEGIN TO LEAVE A MARK, AND I LEAVE MY MARK
IN MANY PEOPLE'S HEARTS."
– RIGOBERTA MENCHÚ TUM

RUTH BADER GINSBURG

Once upon a time, there was a girl who dreamed of becoming a great lawyer. "A lady lawyer?" people would mock her. "Don't be ridiculous! Lawyers and judges are always men."

Ruth looked around her and saw that they were right. "But there's no reason why that shouldn't change," she thought to herself.

She applied to Harvard Law School and became one of its brightest students.

Her husband, Marty, was also a student at Harvard. "Your wife should be home baking cookies and looking after the baby," people used to say. But Marty didn't listen. Ruth was a terrible cook! And besides, he loved taking care of their daughter, and was proud of his brilliant wife.

Ruth was passionate about women's rights and argued six landmark cases on gender equality before the United States Supreme Court. Then she became the second female Supreme Court Justice in the country's history.

There are nine justices on the Supreme Court. "If I'm asked, when will there be enough women on the Supreme Court, I say, 'When there are nine.' People are shocked—but there've been nine men, like forever, and nobody's ever raised their eyebrows at that."

Ruth has never let anything get in the way of her important job on the Supreme Court. Despite her many battles with cancer and multiple surgeries, Ruth rarely missed a day in court—even in her eighties! Ruth is also a style icon, thanks to the extravagant collars she wears in court with her judge's robes.

BORN MARCH 15, 1933
UNITED STATES OF AMERICA

IILLUSTRATION BY
ELEANOR DAVIS

"I DISSENT."
—RUTH BADER GINSBURG

SERAFINA BATTAGLIA

ANTI-MAFIA WITNESS

Serafina owned a coffee shop. Her husband was a criminal. He belonged to a violent organization called the Mafia. He and his friends would meet at her coffee shop to plot all sorts of crimes.

Serafina heard the men plotting, but she never spoke up or tried to stop them. In her twisted world, people who went to the police were despised, while those who robbed and killed were admired.

One fateful day, the men in her husband's gang turned against him. They killed him and Serafina's son. Many other women had seen their loved ones killed, but none of them had spoken out. For Serafina, though, this was too much. She realized that her silence had allowed terrible things to happen.

Wrapped in a mourning shawl, she went to court to face the men accused of killing her son. There, the most powerful Mafia bosses in Italy stood behind bars like animals in a cage. Serafina held the bars and looked the men in the eye. "You drank my son's blood," she said, "and here, before God and man, I spit in your face." And she did. Then she turned to the judge and said, "Mafia bosses have no honor."

That was the start of a ten-year collaboration between Serafina and the police. Thanks to her, officers arrested hundreds of criminals. Some of them later bribed the judges and walked free, but even so, Serafina had set an example. After her, many more women started to speak out.

"If all the women talked about what they know of their men," she said, "the Mafia would no longer exist."

1919–SEPTEMBER 9, 2004
ITALY

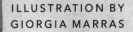
ILLUSTRATION BY
GIORGIA MARRAS

per
Cesare
Terranova

"JUSTICE IS MY WEAPON."
– SERAFINA BATTAGLIA

SOJOURNER TRUTH

Isabella had a powerful voice. But she couldn't use it because she was born into slavery.

When she grew up, Isabella fell in love with a man named Robert and wanted to marry him, but the family who kept him enslaved forbade him from being with her. She was forced to be with another man, Thomas, and they had five children. But Isabella never knew if she would see her children from one day to the next—the slave owners could sell them without even telling her. It was terrifying.

The man who held her captive, Dumont, promised he would set Isabella and her children free, but when the day came, he broke his word. Outraged, Isabella escaped.

Some neighbors who wanted slavery to end paid Dumont twenty dollars, and Isabella was finally set free. Now she could use her voice.

One of her sons, Peter, had been sold to a slave owner in Alabama, but Isabella knew it was illegal to sell slaves across state lines. She took the white man to court and won! Peter returned with her to New York.

Isabella changed her name to Sojourner Truth. "Sojourner" means one who travels, and she set out across the country giving speeches about the true meaning of slavery, and about the importance of equal rights for men and women.

"That man over there says that women need to be helped into carriages, and lifted over ditches . . ." she said in one speech. ". . . Nobody ever helps me into carriages, or over mud-puddles! And ain't I a woman?"

CIRCA 1797–NOVEMBER 26, 1883

UNITED STATES OF AMERICA

"I WILL SHAKE EVERY
PLACE I GO TO."
– SOJOURNER TRUTH

YAA ASANTEWAA

WARRIOR QUEEN

Once upon a time, in a land rich with gold, lived a strong queen who ruled over the Asante kingdom. Her name was Yaa.

Her people believed in the magical powers of a golden stool which was so sacred that even the king and queen were not allowed to touch it. It was said that the heart and soul of the Asante people—past, present, and future—was contained in this golden throne.

One day, a governor-general appointed by the British announced that the British Empire would be taking over the Asante lands. "We also demand your golden stool to sit upon. Bring it here immediately."

The Asante leaders were shocked and insulted—but their enemy was powerful. One by one, they urged surrender.

Not Yaa Asantewaa. She stood up.

"If you, the men of Ashanti, will not go forward, then we, the women, will. We will fight the white men."

Yaa led an army of 5,000 into battle against the well-equipped British soldiers. After a fierce fight, Yaa's army was defeated. She herself was captured and deported to the Seychelles Islands.

She never saw her beloved land again, but her country continued to be inspired by her bravery. A few years after her death, the Asante kingdom regained its independence. To this day, Yaa Asantewaa's people still sing songs about their beloved queen and her proud, fighting spirit.

CIRCA 1840–OCTOBER 17, 1921
GHANA

"IF YOU, THE MEN OF
ASHANTI, WILL NOT
GO FORWARD, THEN
WE WILL. WE, THE
WOMEN, WILL."
—YAA ASANTEWAA

WRITE YOUR STORY

_____

_____

_____

_____

_____

_____

_____

_____

_____

_____

_____

_____

_____

_____

_____

_____

_____

DRAW YOUR PORTRAIT

WHAT KIND OF LEADER ARE YOU?

You, yes YOU, are a leader. Whether loud or quiet, you already have the qualities inside you to lead a revolution. Take this quiz to find out what kind of leader you are!

1. WHEN FACED WITH AN ISSUE, HOW DO YOU SOLVE IT?

    A. I draft a petition and get out my protest sign.
    B. I rally my troops and take my enemies down by any means necessary.
    C. I always solve my problems peacefully and with a cool head.

2. WHICH DESCRIPTION SOUNDS MOST LIKE YOU?

    A. I'm passionate, loud, and feisty.
    B. I'm strong, courageous, and disciplined.
    C. I'm well-spoken, fair, and caring.

3. WHERE WOULD YOU WANT TO LIVE?

    A. I don't need much; anywhere is fine as long as I have a roof over my head.
    B. A lonely castle on the side of a cliff.
    C. A beautiful modern house with too many rooms to count.

4. WHAT'S YOUR FAVORITE FOOD?

    A. Something organic and environmentally friendly
    B. Um . . . pie? Or meat? Possibly a meat pie . . . ?
    C. Something fancy from another culture

5. WHAT DO YOU WISH YOU WERE WEARING RIGHT NOW?

A. A Rebel Girl T-shirt and ripped jeans
B. Full body armor
C. A pantsuit or judge's robes

6. YOU'RE GOING ON AN ADVENTURE! WHERE WILL YOU GO?

A. A country or neighborhood less fortunate than mine
B. Somewhere challenging—like a mountain, desert, or forest
C. A tropical island paradise

7. WHAT AFTER-SCHOOL CLUB WOULD YOU LOVE TO JOIN?

A. Something creative, like drama club, choir, or art club
B. Any sports team—fencing, lacrosse, soccer, tennis—I love them all!
C. The debate team or model U.N.

8. HOW DO YOU MAKE DECISIONS?

A. I follow my heart and the passionate people I care about.
B. It's an even mix between my head and heart.
C. I follow my head and consider the facts.

9. WHAT'S YOUR WEAPON OF CHOICE?

A. The power of the people!
B. A sword or spear
C. My voice and my pen

10. YOU'VE BEEN TRANSPORTED INTO A FAIRY TALE! WHICH CHARACTER WOULD YOU BE?

A. The peasant farmer leading a revolt
B. The hero saving the day
C. The wise old tree giving advice

Check out your results on page 45!

ANSWERS TO "WHAT KIND OF LEADER ARE YOU?"

MOSTLY A'S

You're the Ardent Activist! Your fiery passion mobilizes large groups of people into action that shakes governments and social systems. You might be found at a protest march wielding a creative sign about what you believe in or shouting through a bullhorn with your fist in the air.

MOSTLY B'S

You're the Warrior! Everyone thinks you're bloodthirsty, but really you just want to protect your people and ensure their continued survival. You care very deeply about your community's safety.

MOSTLY C'S

You're the Stately Politician! You are wise beyond your years and you use your knowledge to advise, guide, and coach others around you. You give eloquent speeches full of fire and passion. Each word you speak carries power.

A CONVERSATION WITH ELENA&FRANCESCA

Read about how authors Elena Favilli and Francesca Cavallo lead their company and create their books.

WHAT IS IT LIKE BEING THE MOST POWERFUL PEOPLE IN YOUR COMPANY?

There is a lot of joy, but it's also very tiring. We have to remind ourselves to rest and forgive ourselves if we make mistakes. When you create something new, you make mistakes: that's just the nature of making. What's important is learning from your mistakes and improving before the next go around.

WHY DID YOU DECIDE TO START A BUSINESS?

At first, we wanted to create products that we loved. Then, we wanted to create those products with people that we loved. We wanted to create a work environment where our team members could feel free to express themselves and do the best work of their lives.

WHY DID YOU DECIDE TO WRITE BOOKS?

Stories are what humans are made of. As kids, we understand ourselves and the world around us through stories. Telling someone to do or not do something "because you're a girl" or "because you're a boy" is wrong. Girls can do anything that boys can do. We wrote our books to start changing the story about what it means to be a girl.

WHAT IS YOUR FAVORITE PART OF BEING LEADERS?

Seeing how your work inspires other people is absolutely the best part of being leaders. We are privileged to have an impact on the lives of so many people.

WHAT DO YOU THINK ARE THE STRONGEST QUALITIES OF A GOOD LEADER?

Humility and courage are the most important qualities of a leader. To be a good leader, you also need to be an avid learner. You must adapt quickly and be brave enough to make many decisions every day.

WHO ARE THE FEMALE LEADERS YOU ADMIRE THE MOST?

Our mothers and grandmothers have always been our strongest role models for what it means to be a Rebel Girl. We both come from families with strong women. Women like Serena Williams, Hillary Rodham Clinton, and J. K. Rowling are our role models today.

WHY IS THE WORD "REBEL" IN THE TITLE OF YOUR BOOKS?

We chose the word "rebel" because many girls and women all over the world have to become rebels in order to survive. We encourage girls to learn how to rebel against injustice, because it's an important skill in a woman's life. We feel that the world doesn't need more books inviting women to avoid disagreements. We feel the world needs books inviting women to be themselves, even when this means not being likable.

WHAT IS SPECIAL ABOUT THE ARTWORK IN YOUR BOOKS?

We only hire female artists to illustrate our books. We wanted to show off the amazing work that female artists create every day in every corner of the globe. We also wanted to have a wide variety of art styles so that each woman we wrote about had her own unique personality. Society represents women in a very narrow way, so it was important to show that there is no single way to be a Rebel Girl.

BEING A LEADER

Leaders are powerful. Every leader has to make important decisions that directly impact people who count on them. To do this, they must decide what they believe in, what they support, and who they are. Try these activities below to plan how you will become the next great leader to change the world!

VISUALIZE: *You feel deep inside your soul that you are in the world to make it a better place. You have worked for the entirety of your life to make other people's lives better. You are caring, kind, smart, and you understand how to change bad things you see happening.*

EXERCISE 1:

Write about what makes you powerful.

1. What are you good at? What are your strengths?

_____

_____

2. What issues do you stand for, and what do you believe in?

_____

_____

3. How would you change your community? Your city?
   Your state? The world?

_____

_____

WORKSHOP

EXERCISE 2:

Think about how the women in each story were challenged by the people around them. What makes these women great leaders?

Grace O'Malley (page 17)

_____

_____

Nanny of the Maroons (page 29)

_____

_____

Malala Yousafzai (page 25)

_____

_____

Eufrosina Cruz (page 11)

_____

_____

Sojourner Truth (page 37)

_____

_____

Catherine the Great (page 3)

_____

_____

ILLUSTRATORS

Nineteen extraordinary female artists from all over the world illustrated the portraits in this book. Here are their names!

CRISTINA AMODEO, **ITALY**, 14, 38

ELENIA BERETTA, **ITALY**, 2

SARA BONDI, **ITALY**, 26

MARIJKE BUURLAGE, **NETHERLANDS**, 4

ELEANOR DAVIS, **USA**, 34

ANA GALVAÑ, **SPAIN**, 10

DEBORA GUIDI, **ITALY**, 32

KATHRIN HONESTA, **INDONESIA**, 18

ELENI KALORKOTI, **UK**, 6

JUSTINE LECOUFFE, **USA**, 22

KIKI LJUNG, **BELGIUM**, 8

GIORGIA MARRAS, **ITALY**, 36

SALLY NIXON, **USA**, 20

CAMILLA PERKINS, **USA**, 30

LAURA PÉREZ, **SPAIN**, 16

PAOLA ROLLO, **ITALY**, 12

MARTA SIGNORI, **ITALY**, 28

NOA SNIR, **ISRAEL**, 40

THANDIWE TSHABALALA, **SOUTH AFRICA**, 24

ABOUT THE AUTHORS

Elena Favilli and Francesca Cavallo grew up in Italy. They are *New York Times* bestselling authors whose work has been translated into more than forty-five languages, and they have written for and been reviewed in various publications, including *The Guardian*, *Vogue*, *The New York Times*, *El País*, *The Los Angeles Times*, *Colors Magazine*, *Corriere della Sera*, and *La Repubblica*. They are the founders of Timbuktu Labs, and they live in Venice, California.

Timbuktu Labs is an award-winning media company founded in 2012 by Elena Favilli and Francesca Cavallo. Through a combination of thought-provoking content, stellar design, and business innovation, Timbuktu is redefining the boundaries of indie publishing to inspire a global community of progressive families spanning seventy countries. Timbuktu is home to a diverse and passionate group of rebels who work together in Los Angeles, New York, Atlanta, Mérida (Mexico), London, and Milan.